Will our childre

YOUR CHILD AND DRUGS

Sean Cassin

VERITAS

First published 1999 by
Veritas Publications
7/8 Lower Abbey Street
Dublin 1

ISBN 1 85390 409 0

Design: Bill Bolger
Cover illustration: Angela Hampton Family Life Pictures
© Angela Hampton
Photographs courtesy of the Health Promotion Unit,
Department of Health and Children, Ireland
Printed in Ireland by Betaprint Ltd, Dublin

INTRODUCTION

I often babysit my friends' three children. Their youngest, Adam, was barely a year old when I had to sleep over, do the bottles, the nappies, the lot. That was the easy part. The hard part was not being able to sleep a wink for fear of something going wrong. I was afraid Adam might stop breathing. Early the next morning, I was exhausted after my sleepless night while he was full of life and shouting for his breakfast.

Although his mother assured me that parents grow out of this phase, I was filled with a new appreciation for the way children demand total devotion and generosity of spirit from their parents. Children seem to evoke in parents an instinctive radar that scans the horizon for danger long before it appears. Sometimes our fears and protectiveness for our children can be misplaced, needlessly exhausting us.

The drugs scare creates a lot of these excessive worries for parents. Fear is always about a future unknown and, for many parents, the fears they have about drugs will never be realised. Naturally your fears are aroused when you hear your twelve- or thirteen-year-old talking about ecstasy with some degree of familiarity, but an over-reaction at this time may send the wrong message, giving the child the impression that 'my parents can't cope with the 'e' word so I won't mention it'.

The aim of this booklet is to provide facts about drugs, their attractions and the effects they can have, and to help you reduce, or even prevent, the threat of your child becoming a problem drug user. When you know your facts you have two important controls to help you cope. Firstly, you understand what the various drugs are and what they do, and this will help to reduce some of your fears and enable you to recognise any warning signs. Secondly, you increase your credibility in your child's eyes, which will help him or her to feel that you can be trusted when it comes to talking about drugs.

In writing this booklet, I have tried to answer some of the questions asked repeatedly by parents of drug users. I have worked with drug users and their families in Ireland, London and Rome for the past fifteen years and I have learned that the people with the strongest voice, and the most power to change the problems surrounding drug users, are the family. I am also convinced that the first and most influential step in preventing drug problems is to affirm and impart values to children during their formative years, which will enable them to make the right choices about drugs when the time comes.

CHAPTER 1

Drugs – The Facts

Know The Facts

People will tell you all sorts of things about drugs. You will hear frightening exaggerations, half-truths and sometimes even downright lies. This chapter is designed to give you the plain unvarnished facts. It tells you which drugs you could come across, what they are and what they can do to your child.

Drugs Are Not The Problem, But How They Are Used

It is useful to keep in mind that drugs themselves are neither good nor bad, helpful nor harmful. All the dangers or benefits are in the way they are used. Societies as far back as 3,000 BC have used opium. Every civilisation uses drugs to a greater or lesser extent. Some of these drugs are accepted and some are taboo. In our society, alcohol and tobacco are socially and culturally accepted, while the coca leaf that makes cocaine is accepted in South American countries. The central issue is not the presence or absence of drugs but how they are used.

The Problem With The Black Market

When you buy something from a shop you know that what it says on the wrapper is what you are getting. On the black market you have no guarantee that a drug contains what it is supposed to. To increase the income to the supplier, these drugs are frequently increased in volume by adding sugar, laxatives or cheaper drugs. This means that you can never be sure of the strength of the drug, which can result in overdose or poisoning.

There is increasing support for legally controlling the availability of drugs. The current practice among doctors and chemists of dispensing a synthetic opiate, methadone – which has similar effects to heroin – has become standard practice for treating opiate users. The success of this method is in its reduction of crime by drug users, as they no longer need to steal to buy illegal drugs. This method of medically supervised drug use also helps to prevent dangerous infections such as HIV and hepatitis spreading to drug users, their partners and to society in general. Another advantage of legally controlling commonly used drugs is that it takes the trade away from unscrupulous criminals.

How Do Drugs Work?

Some drugs, such as alcohol, cannabis and tranquillisers, work by reducing the control over the muscles, lessening the brain reaction time and lowering the concentration time. Other drugs, such as cocaine, amphetamines and ecstasy, enhance reaction times and stimulate brain activity.

Taking drugs to relieve depression, anxiety or aggression may provide fleeting relief, but will leave the user feeling worse when the effect wears off.

Mixing drugs, especially depressants like alcohol, solvents or tranquillisers, can make a powerful cocktail so strong it can kill.

Psychological Addiction

Psychological addiction is when someone is convinced that he or she needs to take a drug regularly, and while there may be some anxiety, fear and emotional upset on withdrawal, there are no real physical effects. Cannabis is said to be psychologically addictive in this way.

Physical Addiction

Physical addiction carries all the characteristics of psychological dependence, and also involves physical pain on withdrawal. Excessive alcohol use causes the most serious physical addiction in this sense, and withdrawal can cause sweating, blackouts, convulsions and even death. Barbiturates (sleeping pills) can also cause serious withdrawals when used on a regular basis.

The Specific Facts About Drugs

The following pages list some of the more commonly used drugs: what they are; the effects they can have; and the specific dangers associated with each one.

Tobacco

Tobacco is the most widely-used addictive substance in this country. Smoking 20 cigarettes a day over 40 years means £36,000 goes up in smoke.

Effects

Inhaling cigarette smoke takes tar, nicotine and poisonous gases like carbon monoxide into the body. Some smokers believe that smoking helps them to relax or concentrate, and some believe smoking will keep their weight down. Smoking constricts the blood vessels and decreases the supply of oxygen to the body, causing decreased physical stamina and an increased likelihood of wrinkles. Prolonged smoking can cause lung cancer and cardiovascular disease. The nicotine in tobacco is highly addictive and research has shown that those who begin smoking in their teens find it more difficult to quit than those who begin later. The physical effects of withdrawal last approximately a week, and can include feelings of intense irritability, tension and fatigue along with strong cravings. The psychological craving for cigarettes can last a lot longer.

Alcohol

By eleven years of age most children will have tried alcohol. Alcohol is made from the fermenting of grains, fruits or vegetables. Beer is the product of this fermenting process and it contains about one part alcohol to twenty parts water. Spirits such as whiskey or gin are made by then distilling the fermented juices, resulting in a much higher alcohol content.

Effects

The effects of alcohol begin quickly and can last for several hours. After the first few drinks, people feel less inhibited, more relaxed and more responsive to their surroundings.

For many, drinking can be an enjoyable and sociable experience when done in moderation. Excessive intake of alcohol can lead to loss of balance, speech difficulties, double vision, and unconsciousness. The morning-after hangover can include such symptoms as headaches, dehydration, upset stomach and shakiness. Sustained heavy drinking increases the risk of liver disease, various cancers and ulcers and can lead to cardiovascular disorders and brain damage. Alcohol can become addictive when consumed regularly over a prolonged period of time. The effects of withdrawal include sweating, blackouts, convulsions and even death.

Amphetamines *(speed, uppers, whizz)*

During the sixties, these drugs were prescribed for depression and appetite suppression. Today they are sold on the black market as pills or powder that can be sniffed or injected.

Effects

Amphetamines give the user an energy boost and provide a sense of confidence. This can lead to hyperactivity with an accompanying anxiety, or make the person 'narky' or irritable. As the effects wear off, the user may feel very fatigued, depressed and unusually hungry. It can take a couple of days to recover. With frequent use, amphetamines can become psychologically addictive.

Cocaine *(snow, rock, crack, charlie)*

This is a drug that is similar to amphetamines in that it is a powerful stimulant. It is a white powder made from the leaves of the coca plant. It can be sniffed through a tube into the nostrils or injected and absorbed into the bloodstream. Crack is a diluted form of cocaine. Crack is usually smoked, and its name came from the sound it makes when burning.

Effects

Cocaine gives the brain very exhilarated feelings, with a sense of well-being and indifference to pain and danger. It can give delusions of physical and mental strength. These effects are not always guaranteed and it can also give a 'bad trip' that creates anxiety and feelings of panic. The effects tend to wear off very quickly, which encourages repeated use in shorter and shorter spaces of time. Long-term use can leave the user feeling sick, unable to sleep and can also cause weight loss. Continuous sniffing damages the membranes in the nose.

This drug is said to be 'psychologically addictive' which means withdrawal causes mental and emotional cravings rather than physical reactions to the absence of the drug.

Ecstasy ***(Es, Denis the Menace, Mad Bastards, Love Doves, Disco Burgers, Phase 4)***

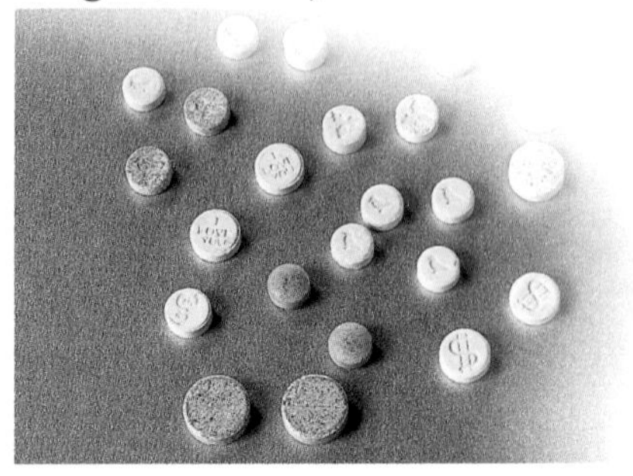

Ecstasy can come in tablet form, as coloured capsules, liquid or powder. In Ireland it is mostly sold in tablet form. It contains some amphetamine and other natural herbs and organic compounds.

Effects

Ecstasy arouses friendly and sociable feelings towards others. It can also increase the user's energy levels. For this reason the drug became popular with young people who also liked the types of dance music (e.g. house, techno, garage, jungle, etc.) and the lifestyle associated with 'the rave scene'. This is music with more emphasis on a pounding rhythm than on lyrics. 'Raves' were clandestine in the early days but have since become mainstream. Young people can dance for hours assisted by the 'speedy' qualities of ecstasy. Because the drug can take at least half an hour to work, some users repeat the dose within half an hour as they think the drug is not having any effect. If too much is taken it can lead to anxiety, confusion or paranoia. Ecstasy affects the body's ability to control temperature. When taken in a hot atmosphere like at raves it can contribute to heat stroke and this has resulted in several deaths. It's important to avoid either too little or too much body fluid. The risks can be reduced if users:

- chill out regularly;
- sip up to a pint of non-alcoholic fluids like fruit juice or water, every hour.

When the effects wear off, not surprisingly there can be feelings of tiredness and sadness or sheer exhaustion. Some users have resorted to smoking heroin to counteract these low feelings. Regular users have difficulty sleeping and some women have more difficult periods. There is growing evidence to suggest that ecstasy may harm certain brain cells which control moods and so leave the user prone to depression. Long-term use can lead to liver damage. It's not clear whether the withdrawal discomfort after use is due to the fatigue from hyperactivity or due to the absence of the drug. Regular use can create psychological dependence.

LSD ***(acid, trips)***

This is a chemically designed drug (lysergic acid diethylamide) that is impregnated onto blotting paper in minute quantities. It is sold as tiny squares with attractive colour designs which are dissolved on the tongue.

Effects

LSD has a hallucinogenic effect on the brain, resulting in the user seeing things that are not there, increased sensory awareness, and a distorted or heightened perception of sound and time. The pleasant effects depend on the mood of the person, where they are and who they are with. Bad trips can lead to depression, dizziness or panic. This is more likely if the user is in unfamiliar surroundings. There are no real addictive or withdrawal effects from LSD.

Magic Mushrooms

These small mushrooms grow wild in untilled fields and woodlands from September well into November. They can be boiled and eaten as a soup, dried or eaten whole. The most common type are called Liberty Caps as they have a bell-like shape.

Effects

Magic mushrooms have much the same effect as LSD, except much higher quantities are required to feel the effects and they take longer to work. They distort perceptions and so it can be risky to drive or negotiate traffic, even if walking. There can be an unpredictable recurrence of the trip or hallucination a day or two after taking them. Another danger is that they may be confused with poisonous varieties of mushrooms. They don't have any real addictive qualities.

Cannabis *(dope, blow, grass, hash, ganjha)*

The cannabis plant was once used to make hemp fibres. It is used to produce cannabis resin, called hash, which is compressed into transportable blocks. Marijuana is another product of the plant, which is made by drying the leaves and seeds. Both of these can be rolled into cigarettes by mixing them with tobacco. Cannabis can also be mixed into various foods and drinks, e.g. 'hash cakes' and 'space cookies'.

Effects

Cannabis can make people feel more relaxed and talkative. It reduces the ability to carry out complicated tasks, which means that it's dangerous to drive while under the influence of this drug. Inexperienced people taking high doses or using it while depressed or anxious can make their condition worse or bring on panic attacks. Like tobacco, smoking this drug carries a higher risk of cancer and can also cause breathing disorders. The drug is not physically addictive but it can cause a psychological reliance on its use similar to a physical craving for the drug.

SOLVENTS

Solvents are found in products like glue, lighter fuel, paint, aerosol sprays and petrol. When the vapours are inhaled the effect is similar to that of alcohol. Some people increase the effect by inhaling from inside a plastic bag placed around the face. Aerosol cans can be used by placing a handkerchief over the outlet to filter the contents other than the solvent.

Effects

Using solvents creates an effect like being drunk and it includes the hangover. The inhaled vapours are absorbed by the lung tissue and quickly reach the brain. Excessive inhaling can cause loss of control over the body. Some users have sniffed to the point of being unconscious and then choked on their own vomit. In some cases sudden activity after inhaling can over-strain the heart, causing a heart attack. For this reason it is dangerous to chase someone who has been sniffing solvents. Some first time users have died as a result of squirting aerosol gases directly into their mouths, causing a freezing of the air passages. Repeated use of solvents creates a psychological dependence but there are no real physical withdrawal symptoms.

BARBITURATES *(downers, sleepers, barbs)*

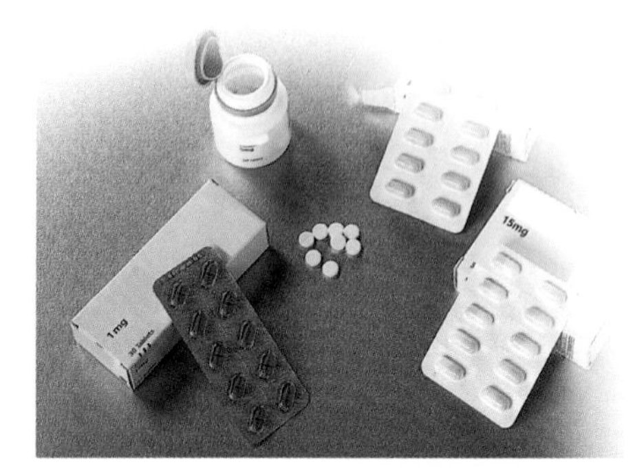

Barbiturates have a calming effect and are only available by prescription. They are mostly found as a powder in coloured capsules. Most users will swallow them, sometimes with alcohol to boost their effects, and some inject them.

Some of the trade names for these drugs are Seconal, Tuinal, and Nembutal.

Effects

Some young ecstasy users take barbiturates to combat the effects of irritability, tension and exhaustion that follow a night of dancing at a rave. When taken regularly, these drugs can make a user very dependent on them. This means that increased doses are needed just to feel normal. It also means that trying to stop can be acutely distressing and painful. Sudden withdrawal is so dangerous that the convulsions can cause death. For these reasons they are particularly dangerous drugs.

TRANQUILLISERS *(trancs, benzos, jellies)*

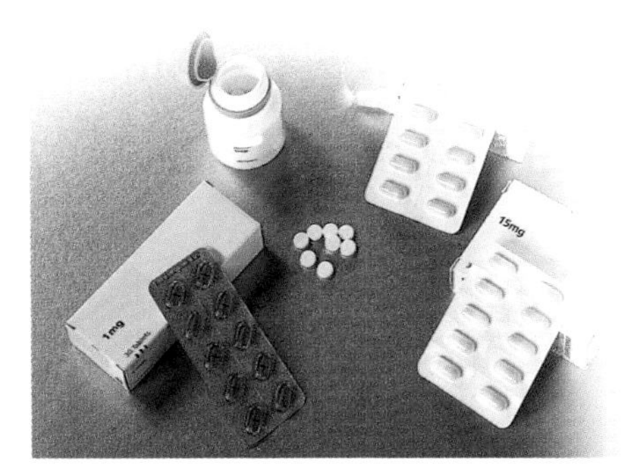

Tranquillisers have a milder effect than barbiturates. They are prescribed by doctors to reduce tension, calm people down or help them to sleep. Valium, Librium, Dalmane and Attivan are some of the trade names by which these drugs are known.

Effects

People who feel tense and anxious can become calm and relaxed. Drug users take them to increase the effects of other drugs like alcohol or heroin, or to calm them down after the use of 'speedy' drugs like amphetamines, cocaine or ecstasy. They can create a dependence when taken regularly and while the withdrawals are not as serious as those associated with barbiturates they can still be distressing.

HEROIN *(smack, gear, junk, skag, H)*

Heroin was first made from morphine in 1874. It wasn't used for medicinal purposes until the beginning of this century, when its effectiveness in relieving pain made it popular. Pure heroin originates from the opium poppy and is very white in colour and bitter to the taste. Black market heroin can range from white to brown in colour because of impurities left from manufacturing it. Pure heroin is rarely sold on the street. A bag of heroin, also known as 'Q' (for quarter gram), would fit on the nail of your index finger. It's seldom a quarter gram and is diluted frequently to five per cent heroin, often less. It can be smoked and this is called 'chasing the dragon'. The heroin is heated on tinfoil and the smoke is inhaled. Most users prefer injecting it as the effects are stronger and more immediate, providing more value for money.

Effects

The pain relief properties of heroin can be accompanied by a tremendous sense of euphoria. Sometimes the first reaction to taking heroin is nausea. Under its influence the pupils contract to the size of a pin-point (pinned), and there's a reduction in physical activity. Large doses can cause drowsiness, which may induce sleep. This sleepy behaviour is known as 'goofing'. Overdose is indicated by nausea, vomiting and a slowing down in the breathing rate.

Repeated use of the drug creates both a psychological and a physical dependence. Withdrawal is not as painful as from alcohol or barbiturates, but can seem intense to users as their pain thresholds become very low from taking this drug. The use of methadone, a human-made opiate, can control these withdrawals.

Heroin injectors need to have access to clean needles, syringes and sterile swabs to avoid infecting themselves and others. Most heroin injectors will have stopped using by their early thirties, or sooner. For this reason, every effort needs to be made to keep them healthy, so they are alive to make this decision when the time comes. One way to help is to support local services that provide needle exchanges and health services for injecting drug users.

CHAPTER 2

Prevention Is Better Than Cure

Can Parents Do Anything?

Yes!

There are two things that you can do to prevent drugs becoming a problem for your child:

- Teach them life skills such as valuing themselves and other people.
- Give them the facts about drugs.

Teaching Values

As a parent you can help build a strong immune system for your child. The following are five basic things that children need to prepare them to be self-reliant in later years, which will help to reduce the likelihood of their becoming reliant on drugs.

1 Physical care and protection
2. Affection and approval
3. Stimulation and teaching
4. Disciplines and controls suited to the child's age and level of development
5. Encouragement to take gradual control over their own lives

As children get older, the behaviours they choose will certainly be influenced by the way their parents behaved towards them in their younger years. Drugs and alcohol are very powerful ways of relieving hurt and angry feelings. They give an illusory sense of self-worth that is better, at least for a little while, than the reality of feeling inadequate, a failure or a misfit.

Many of the drug users in recovery will recount early childhood grievances which fit into four categories:

1. Being punished for positive behaviours like smiling, manipulating for what they wanted or needed, being mobile (running, jumping, climbing).
2. Being pushed away or discouraged from bonding with parents. This leaves problems later with negotiating intimacy, being comforted and receiving affection.
3. Being constantly criticised. This leaves children with damaged self-esteem which can make the approval of low achievers they meet later seem wonderful. (Young women and men who got involved in prostitution to earn drug money spoke of their misplaced sense of being valued and needed by those who used them.)
4. Overprotective parents who always disapproved of their friends. If their qualities of friendliness and social skills had been encouraged when they were children it would have helped them cope with the very lonely feelings they experienced in early adolescence.

Ten Commandments

The following are my Ten Commandments for developing a strong immune system in your child:

I. Use affection as the basis for discipline

Drug use is often a substitute for the warm feelings that affectionate relationships provide. The more you accompany 'no' and 'can't' with explanations that show care and affection, the more positive the response from your child will be.

II. Set limits

I once facilitated a group with a father and his son who was getting off drugs. The father was quite wealthy and asked his son how he could have done this to his parents. What especially upset the father was that he had given his son everything he had asked for: when his son was unhappy at school and asked to change to his friend's school, his father said yes; when he asked for a motor bike he said yes; when he asked for more pocket money he said yes. His son, who was crying in acknowledgement of his ingratitude, said through his anguish, 'yes, yes, yes, but you never taught me how to cope with saying no'. When his son was introduced to drugs and alcohol and the attraction of the highs, his instinct was to say yes, almost from habit. Setting limits does not mean constant investigation of and intrusion on your children, but it does mean saying no to them at times.

III. Show you bother by being a bother

Children can interpret a parent's happy-go-lucky approach as lack of interest. Often adolescents provoke their parents as a way of measuring their strength of feeling for them. It's good to show that you do bother about your children by being a bother to them at times.

IV. Making rules helps

Learning rules helps children to understand that there are rules in society which will help them to get on with other people and to achieve things. Rules should be clear, firm and reasonable. Some useful rules for children are that they tell you where they are and who they are with.

V. Family routines teach shortcuts for living

Recently a twenty-five-year-old asked if he could come in to our High Park 'live in' facility to withdraw from his alcohol and drug use. He said it was the dirt that got to him in the end. Living in hostels, being broke and not being able to wash himself every morning became unbearable. Once learned, the family routines of washing, mealtimes and bedtime become lifelong disciplines. Apart from the safe and secure feelings these routines generate, they enable an easier adjustment to school discipline and its dependence on routines. Early school leaving has the highest incidence of problem drug use. A great deal of this early leaving stems from the lack of home routines. Recently, some Dublin schools found that low performance in children stemmed from their hunger, as they had no breakfasts before coming to school. Your home routines of bath, bed, and prayers aren't trivial but are strong ways for children to learn survival skills.

VI. Be consistent

Try, where possible, to apply the same rules over time. What was established as fair yesterday needs to apply today and tomorrow too. Children and adolescents need the continuity of consistency as a kind of stockade or defence from their own worst anarchies.

VII. Be persistent

Children of all ages need to test limits and to see if sufficient rebellion, tantrums or cajoling can change their parents' position. If you are frequently giving in to your children's unreasonable demands you send messages that your word is inconsistent and that with sufficient pressure parents will give way.

VIII. Children do need to know

As adults it's far easier for us to obey rules when we know the reasons for them. To constantly demand of children that they obey simply because you say so may get compliance out of fear but it won't help them to internalise the value of the rule. When adolescents know both the pleasures and the dangers of drugs they are far more likely to avoid injury to themselves from drug use. The 'Just Say No' slogan is a bit too mindless for most teenagers as it lacks the internalised values about *why* they need to say no.

IX. Attend to the positives

Emphasise to your children the things they should do, more often than telling them what they shouldn't do. Attending to the positives makes children more likely to repeat them. Children will get a natural high out of achieving positive things, and praise for these achievements adds to their good feelings. If a child learns how to achieve natural positive 'highs', then the positive effects of drug use will seem less attractive when weighed against the negative effects. Encouraging your children to pray and to develop a spirituality that can wonder at God's presence and His creation enhances their positive feelings about themselves and others.

X. Children need to be both heard and seen

The saying about children being seen and not heard is not very good advice, as children need to be understood as much as adults do. Being able to listen to your child with respect is a skill which will be very rewarding later. Look for the hidden messages in his or her acting out, made-up stories, or fantasy friends, as these are often a child's way of trying to communicate with others about his or her world. When you notice and respond to these messages, you strengthen your child's willingness to communicate, and affirm enormously his or her sense of self-worth.

Give The Facts

There is no substitute for establishing at an early age the kind of relationship where your child feels free to ask you questions and can count on answers that are both understandable and honest. The earlier that parents create these channels of talk and trust, the easier it is to sustain this communication into the adolescent years.

Some parents think that to talk to their five-year-old about drugs will rob the child too soon of his or her childhood or, worse, put ideas into his or her head that will actually encourage drug use.

The same arguments have been used to oppose sex education for children and these notions fly in the face of the facts. Research has shown that children who have had sex education will have sexual intercourse at a later age than those who have had no sex education.

Similarly, government education programmes in England have shown that early drug education can delay dabbling in illegal substances. In 1991 and 1992 the Home Office evaluated a programme called Project Charlie, run in Hackney, England. The content of this programme was similar to our own life skills programmes, which teach young children in school how to stay healthy and how to stay safe. They emphasise ways to stay well and how to value yourself, rather than giving fear messages or just giving the facts on their own. A follow-up study showed big differences between the drug use of children who had done the programme and the drug use of those who had not. Four years after the course the children involved were shown to:

- have greater skills in resisting peer pressure;
- have more negative attitudes towards drugs;
- be less likely to have used illegal drugs and tobacco.

Talking to your child about drugs will enable him or her to absorb what your own views are as a parent and to ask you those vexing 'why' questions. Later, when your child reaches adolescence, he or she will be more likely to talk to you about drugs if you have lain the 'talking platform' at an earlier stage.

How To Talk To Your Child About Drugs

The most effective way to educate your child about drugs is to give him or her the facts on a gradual basis. There are two kinds of facts to impart in order to demonstrate to your child that he or she can look to you as a source of reliable information. Firstly, talk about what drugs are, what they're made of and why people take them: the short-term effects are often pleasurable, mind-altering and energising. Don't hide these facts as your child is likely to have heard something about drugs already and is counting on you to be honest. Secondly, talk about the damage that drugs can do. It's better to avoid telling scare stories as they only present your own fears.

Teach your child about other drugs, such as alcohol and medicine. For example, explain about the social side of drinking as well as the negative side of drinking too much. An example of how you had to limit your own drinking in order to drive home is a vivid way of sending the right message to a child.

If you have medicine in the house, explain that all medicines are drugs, but not all drugs are medicines. Encourage simple safety rules in your house, and explain that only a grown-up like a parent or doctor can handle medicine because a mistake could be dangerous. Household items like solvents, glues and aerosols can be used as drugs. Explain that these are dangerous and should be treated with caution.

Ask your child what drug or alcohol education he or she is getting in school. Some parents hope that the school will carry the main burden for training their children in safety practices about health, relationships, drugs, etc. The schools can't do it alone. Do join parent associations and clubs that include the drug issue on their agenda. The stronger the coping and prevention measures are in your area, the more supportive the environment will be for your child.

Some Don'ts

Don't threaten

We already looked at the way our fears about drugs can make us overprotective towards our children. The problem, particularly with teenagers, is that they will resist your protective fear as it reminds them of how they were treated as babies. It's no longer effective to say, 'I'm warning you, don't touch that, it's dangerous'.

Avoid extreme views

Don't favour liberal experimentation with drugs or, on the other hand, try not to be extremely against all drugs.

Do not over-react

For example, to respond to a once-off smoke of hash or an ecstasy tablet taken out of curiosity with statements like 'my child is a drug addict' is over-reacting.

Avoid asking too many questions

Don't question intensely what your child's drug experiences may or may not be. Questioning like this often makes children more defensive and secretive about what they do.

Don't over-dramatise

Avoid sifting through sensational newspaper stories that show the most dramatic horror stories about drugs as a way of teaching your child.

CHAPTER 3

What Should I Do If My Child Uses Drugs?

It helps to remember your own early teenage years and what kind of drugs you dabbled in, in order to get some perspective on what your child may do. In your time, the drugs available were very different from those available now and were probably legal. If your own parents found that you had taken alcohol, for example, it was probably not grounds for calling you an alcoholic and rushing you into a treatment programme. Some parents contact us here at Merchants' Quay in a very anxious state because they found out their adolescent was smoking hash or had taken ecstasy. It often turns out that the young person took a smoke of cannabis or ecstasy on just one occasion simply 'to see what it was like'.

Like your own experimentation with drugs, you need to gauge whether it's just a curiosity thing, whether it's more frequent dabbling or if it's consistent use over time with a range of accompanying behavioural and emotional problems.

The following are descriptions of the three main categories of drug use and some appropriate responses, which may be helpful in deciding on the best approach for you to use:

The Experimenter

By the age of eleven most children will have tasted alcohol; by fourteen they will at least know someone who smokes hash and will be curious to try ecstasy. This is the experimental stage and for the vast majority it stops with the experiment. They either get sick from the alcohol, get nothing from the cannabis or ecstasy, or simply enjoy it but know enough to decide on their own limits.

WHAT TO DO

The important thing at this stage is to encourage your child to talk about the experience, try to understand how he or she felt about it, answer his or her questions and affirm his or her positive decision to leave the experiment behind and to learn from it. Remember that occasional use of small amounts of alcohol, cannabis, or even ecstasy won't do any damage. It's only persistent use that will begin to cause problems.

I recently met with a couple who had phoned me in great distress. Their fourteen-year-old had come home from a friend's birthday party acting drunk. She told her mother that she hadn't been drinking but had smoked a 'joint' (a marijuana cigarette). When I spoke to the child on her own, she said it had made her feel sick as well as 'stoned' and she asked me if I could do something to calm her parents down as she had no intention of doing it again.

THE DABBLER

The behaviour of the dabbler is one that warrants your attention in a different way.

Many pre-adolescents will dabble in some drug use. This consists of more regular use than the once-off taste of whiskey or the coughing experiment with cigarettes. It can also include more frequent use of drugs such as cannabis, magic mushrooms or ecstasy.

More serious dabbling consists of frequent use over a limited period. Many teenagers will go to cider parties, lager parties or raves in the summer holidays, when they have the money. These involve using greater quantities of alcohol, cannabis or ecstasy.

The problems associated with this dabbling are mainly the effects produced by the drugs at the time they're taken.

It's easy enough for your child or adolescent to conceal this kind of dabbling, as his or her behaviour quickly returns to normal after the event. However, the day-after hangover will give you some indication of any drug use, and in the case of ecstasy use, an excessive exhaustion accompanied with irritability and nervous agitation are clues, though not absolutes.

Most children who dabble in drugs do not become addicted but research in England has shown that almost one in seven will become a regular user.

What To Do

When in doubt check it out

The presence of physical evidence indicating drug use, such as tablets, alcohol bottles, burned spoons or brown resin-like stains from cannabis, affords a good opportunity for opening up the issue. Being confronted with the physical evidence has a powerful impact in mirroring back to the user the realities of his or her drug use. Simply saying 'this looks like a drug so can you explain what it is?' is a good starting point.

Another opening for discussion is to comment on the behavioural changes you have witnessed. If your child appeared drunk or stoned or buzzing in a way that was uncharacteristic, simply repeat back to him the next day what he said or how he looked and moved. If he was stoned you might say his speech was sounding as if his tongue was sticking to his mouth or that his eyes were nodding off in the middle of the day.

Avoid asking questions that can prompt any denials as these only reinforce the user's own belief that nothing is wrong. For example, the question 'were you smoking hash in your room last night?' prompts an instantly defensive 'no' answer. Questions that seek an explanation of facts are better than questions that evoke excuses about behaviour. Ask for an explanation of the strange hash smell from the bedroom or the change in speech pattern to a slower than normal drawl.

Avoid tackling issues while your child is under the influence of the drug. The behaviours that accompany most drug use are different from a person's natural behaviour and often include a kind of indifference to the realities around him, making him unlikely to feel any of the impact of what you are saying. Wait until he has returned to normal.

One mother of a teenager became fed up of her son constantly missing school on Mondays. Exhausted after the weekend raves and de-motivated from smoking too many joints, he would stay in bed until midday or later. His mother tried calling him repeatedly, opening the windows, playing the radio full-blast, but to no avail. I was amused when she told me she even sat on the cornflakes to prevent her son having his breakfast at lunch time. In the end she offered him a choice. He could come home and get up for school the next morning, or not come home if he wasn't going to get up for school. After testing his mother's nerves by staying out once, she calmly asked him if his return home indicated his choice to go to school. It did and he completed his Leaving Certificate the following year.

The Regular User

The regular user will invariably use on a daily basis. He or she will feel the need to take his or her drug of preference in order to feel normal. This state takes some time to arrive at and needs to be worked on. In the case of ecstasy use, it develops from using alcohol or sleepers or perhaps a smoke of heroin to offset the feelings of exhaustion, irritability and agitation following the rave and ecstasy use of the night before. This pattern of drug use to avoid the pain of the after-effects becomes extended into the week in a gradual way until the person is using on a daily basis 'just to feel normal'. It's important to remember that when regular users can't get the drug they prefer they will use any drug they can get in order to reduce cravings and ward off withdrawal sickness.

The regular user is sometimes referred to as a compulsive user or as being addicted, but these terms aren't very useful with younger users as they tend to create an idea in parents' minds that the user can't help himself. Compulsion and addiction are terms that suggest a loss of control and give the impression that the drug is in the driving seat. This is not usually the case with younger users who at the very least have some power of decision over their choices even if this is weakened by the drug's attractiveness.

It is better for parents to avoid labelling the behaviour as an addiction and instead to focus on the individual choices the user is making and needs to make in order to tackle the issue of his or her drug use. This gives parents a better attitude to cope with what is a frightening and seemingly uncontrollable upset to the whole family.

Most young users will hold for a good many years to the belief that they 'can quit tomorrow' and it's this belief that needs to be most strongly challenged in getting them to face and change their behaviour.

One of the more moving interventions I witnessed was that of a parent couple whose youngest son was in prison, on remand for a charge of possession of heroin with intent to supply. When they visited him in prison, he begged them to pay bail for his release until the court hearing. His mother told him that she and her husband had talked this over with his brother and sister and they had all agreed they could spend no more time or money on trying to solve his problems. They had already borrowed money to send him to a treatment programme which he didn't finish. She said that it seemed to them that the more they did for him the less he did for himself. His father, who wanted to pay the bail, admitted as much to his son, but said that he realised he would be a stronger father if he insisted on his son taking responsibility for his own life. Later, when I visited the son in prison, he told me that it was this refusal of his parents that shocked him into his decision not to use drugs again, regardless of the outcome of his court case. With a reduction in his charge to simple possession, he got probation and came directly into our detox and rehab programme in High Park.

What To Do

Overt don't covert!

The trauma and upset of discovering a regular user in the family can send you into a fear and shame corner that leads you to hide the issue from everyone. Indeed, I knew a mother who for two years tried to deny to herself the reality of her fifteen-year-old son's robbing, drinking, and drug-taking. She could not accept it and so avoided owning what was happening even when her wedding ring went missing.

The other hiding tendency is to keep the truth about the drug use from a partner or from brothers and sisters in the family. Often a drug user will confide in a sympathetic parent but lock them into a 'please don't tell Daddy' agreement that only serves to divide the family and create a safe place for the user to hide his or her habit.

Put your fears and facts out to the whole family at every

opportunity and say clearly 'this is our problem, what are we going to do now?'

Mobilise don't paralyse!

Fear and shame can also make you freeze into a kind of inactivity that is preoccupied with blaming, complaining and explaining. Parents often rush into self-blaming, asking tortuously where they went wrong. This leads to a kind of paralysis where the parent seeks to take the responsibility away from the drug user's own choices, and only results in feelings of failure that block any helpful actions being taken.

The urge to explain away even the most awful actions of a drug user in the family is quite common. His or her behaviour is sometimes explained in the most irrational ways such as 'he didn't really mean to rob my wages' or 'she was always such an attention seeker'. It's very natural to seek explanations for behaviour that upsets or even shocks us. It's a way of making its awfulness more bearable or understandable. However, it's more useful to ask what can be done to remedy the situation, and to declare a red line below which the behaviour of any family member is not acceptable.

Sacrificing the family

The challenge to the family in coping with a drug user is in finding the balance. Some parents become so involved in helping the drug user that they end up neglecting the needs of the rest of the family or, at the other extreme, some adopt banishment approaches that render the drug user homeless, more likely to use drugs in a chaotic way and more in danger of infections, overdose and criminal activity.

Negotiating the balance between these extremes is difficult

and is better facilitated with an outside helper. This helper can be a friend who can talk with all the family involved, although a counsellor or family worker from one of the many agencies, either statutory or voluntary, is a better option. A counsellor will seek to gain the agreement of the family on what they are going to cope with and where they will draw the line. The drug user's presence is a key requirement in arriving at a family position.

One family I know will tolerate their son injecting drugs provided he gets clean injecting equipment, doesn't use drugs in the house and respects the property and needs of the other family members. Another family will agree to hold and to dispense their daughter's methadone to support her living more normally and to reduce the risk of her injecting or being involved in crime to get drugs.

What to do in an emergency

Stay calm! If the person seems to be sleeping and doesn't respond to being called or gentle shaking, he may be unconscious. Make sure he is lying on his side so that if he gets sick, he won't choke on vomit. Call a doctor or ambulance. He may then recover but it's better to be safe than sorry.

CHAPTER 4

TREATMENT

Information about treatment for the regular user can be obtained through an informed family doctor or a drugs counsellor. All the local Health Boards have addiction services. It is important to remember that treatment should never be a simple handing over of the problem to someone else. If possible, the issues surrounding problem drug use are best tackled within the context of the family as a whole.

Many drug users find it helpful to do an in-patient programme where they are confined to a hospital for the duration of the treatment process, which can take up to three months. The advantage of the residential or confined facility is that it can provide more support with less likelihood of reverting to drug use when the withdrawals are at their worst. Detoxification is the easiest part of becoming drug free, and many users can do this repeatedly. The biggest challenge is in staying off drugs. A minority of users need longer residential programmes to help them to stay drug free. Programmes like the Merchant's Quay Project and Coolemine enable users to stay for over a year, in order to help them to examine their behaviours and to learn new ways of coping with life. All programmes advocate and usually provide parallel support programmes for parents. This involves attending a group once a week or once a fortnight, where parents can learn from the experiences of others and find support during difficult times.

What Does Treatment Involve?

Treatment involves three stages, during which the user's dependency on drugs is gradually reduced:

The Harm Reduction Stage

This stage begins with acknowledging the drug user's problem, and recognising the fact that, for the present, he will continue using. Treatment at this stage involves providing the user with sterile equipment, such as clean needles. These can be obtained through the Needle Exchange scheme, or from most local pharmacies.

The Maintenance/Detoxification Stage

During this stage, a doctor gives prescribed amounts of a similar drug to the user's drug of choice. Methadone, a synthetic opiate, is prescribed for heroin users, and is taken orally in gradually reducing doses. Users should be allowed to take the substitute drug for as long as they think is necessary, as it means they can lead normal lives and work without having to rob or worry about where their next fix is coming from. This is called maintenance. Some users will take illegal drugs while on this maintenance, but the majority stay stable for longer periods. A doctor may need to increase the daily dosage to help the user get over 'unstable' periods. Some families take responsibility for administering these doses, which helps the user to stick to the correct amount each day. Most drug users, if they are able, should be encouraged to take responsibility for their own treatment programme. It is they who know best what level of medication they need to remain stable and they should be consulted about this, as opposed to having the professionals taking all the responsibility, thereby leaving the user in a perpetual dependency relationship.

This stage requires a lot of support, not only for the drug user, but for other family members as well. It is important to remember that the life of the illegal drug user can be very action-packed and when this stops, it can leave a huge vacuum in its place. For this reason, training workshops that meet their needs are vitally important, along with creative outlets such as outings, fitness training, etc.

Rehabilitation

At this stage, the drug user is ready to withdraw from the prescribed substitute drug. The majority of drug-users do this withdrawal on their own without the help of agencies. A high number become drug free by attending programmes on a daily or even weekly basis, and these are referred to as 'out-patients'.

WHERE TO GET HELP

Voluntary Drug Treatment Centres

Often nowadays your local GP will either advise or directly treat drug users. For more information phone The Merchants' Quay Project at 6771128, 6790044 or contact them on email at HYPERLINK mailto:info@mqp.ie or call the Drugs Helpline at 1-800-459-459. Alternatively, there are many treatment facilities around the country and some of their phone numbers are listed below:

Treatment Facility	Contact/Telephone
Carlow	
Community Alcohol Treatment Service St Dympna's Hospital, Carlow	(0503) 31106
St Francis Farm Drug-Free Residential Training Tullow, Carlow	(0503) 51369
Clare	
Bushypark Treatment Centre Ennis	(065) 40944
Clare Care Ennis	(065) 28178
Narcotics Anonymous Clare	(065) 89194
Cork	
Alcoholics Anonymous	(021) 500481
Anchor Outpatient Treatment Centre Spa Glen, Mallow	(022) 42559
Arbour House Douglas Road, Cork	(021) 968933
Matt Talbot House Garryvoe	(021) 667415

Narcotics Anonymous	(021) 278411
Psychiatric Unit Cork University Hospital, Wilton	(021) 546400
St Helen's Blarney	(021) 382041
St Stephen's Hospital Glanmire	(021) 821411
Tabor Lodge Belgooly	(021) 887110

Donegal

North Western Health Board Letterkenny	(074) 28769 (075) 21044 (077) 61500 (073) 21933
St Conal's Hospital Letterkenny	(074) 21022

Dublin

Alcoholics Anonymous Dublin 8	(01) 453 8998/679 5967
Alcoholics Anonymous (Family Support) Dublin 1	(01) 873 2699
Alcohol Rehabilitation Centre Dublin 2	(01) 677 3232
Ana Liffey Drug Project Dublin 1	(01) 878 6899
Ballymun Youth Action Project Ballymun	(01) 842 8071
Central Addiction Service Dublin 2	(01) 677 1122
Clondalkin Addiction Support Programme Clondalkin	(01) 623 0770

Community Addiction Counselling	
Ballyfermot	(01) 626 2547
Ballymun	(01) 842 0011
Castle Street, Dublin 2	(01) 475 7837
Raheny, Dublin 5	(01) 848 0666
Rathdown Park, Dublin 7	(01) 868 0444 ext. 144
Dun Laoghaire	(01) 280 8471
Tallaght	(01) 451 3894
Community Alcohol Services	
Tallaght	(01) 451 6589
Coolmine House	
Lord Edward Street, Dublin 2	(01) 679 3765
Cuan Dara Detoxification Unit	
Ballyfermot	(01) 623 5817
Eastern Health Board	
Satellite Clinic	
Amiens Street, Dublin 1	(01) 874 9360
Cherry Orchard, Dublin 10	(01) 626 2476
Baggot Street, Dublin 4	(01) 660 2149/2227
Specialist Addiction Service	
Pearse Street, Dublin 2	(01) 671 7659
Mater Dei Counselling Centre	
Clonliffe Road, Dublin 3	(01) 837 1892
Merchant's Quay Project: Drugs/HIV Service	
Merchant's Quay, Dublin 8	(01) 679 0044
Narcotics Anonymous	
Cardiff Lane, Dublin 2	(01) 830 0944 ext. 486
Narcotics Anonymous (Family Support)	
Upper Gardiner Street, Dublin 1	(01) 874 8431
Rialto Community Drug Team	
Rialto, Dublin 6	(01) 454 0021
Rutland Centre	
Templeogue, Dublin 16	(01) 494 6358
SAOL Women's Project	(01) 855 3393

Soilse
Henrietta Place, Dublin 1 (01) 872 4922

Stanhope Centre
Lower Grangegorman, Dublin 7 (01) 677 3965

Talbot Centre
Upper Buckingham Street, Dublin 1 (01) 836 3434

Teen Counselling
Clondalkin, Dublin 22 (01) 623 1398

Springfield, Dublin 24 (01) 462 3083

GALWAY

Addiction Counselling Service
Ballinasloe (0905) 44103

Loughrea (091) 847003

Tuam (093) 24695

Alcoholics Anonymous (01) 453 8998

Alcoholism Counselling Service
Merlin Park Regional Hospital (091) 753595

Community Addiction Counselling Service
Mountbellow (0905) 79571

Cuan Mhuire
Athenry (091) 797102

Horizon House
Barna (091) 591812

Narcotics Anonymous
Galway (091) 756404

KERRY

General Hospital
Tralee (066) 26222

Talbot Grove Treatment Centre
Castle Island (066) 41511

Kildare

Community Addiction Counselling Naas	(045) 876001
Cuan Mhuire Athy	(0507) 31090

Kilkenny

Community Alcohol Treatment Service St Luke's Hospital, Kilkenny	(056) 63677
Sr Veronica Adolescent Residential Centre Ballyraggett, Kilkenny	(056) 33114

Laois

Alcohol and Drugs Counselling Services Portlaoise	(0502) 21364 ext. 409

Limerick

Churchtown Day Hospital Newcastle	(069) 61799
Cuan Mhuire Bruree	(063) 90555/90505/90545
Franciscan Friary Limerick	(061) 413911
Kilmallock Day Hospital Limerick	(063) 98668
Narcotics Anonymous Henry Street, Limerick	(061) 314111
St Anne's Day Hospital Roxboro Road, Limerick	(061) 315177
'Tevere' Day Hospital Shelbourne Road, Limerick	(061) 452971
Willowdale Day Hospital Shelbourne Road, Limerick	(061) 302248

Longford

Community Alcohol and Drugs Services St Mel's Road, Longford	(043) 46827

Louth

Alcoholism Counselling Service Ardee	(041) 53264
Community Services Centre Drogheda	(041) 36084
Dundalk Counselling Centre Dundalk	(042) 38333

Mayo

Addiction Counselling Service St Mary's Hospital, Castlebar	(094) 21733
Hope House Foxford	(094) 56888

Meath

Community Alcohol and Drugs Services Mullingar	(044) 48289
St Loman's Hospital Mullingar	(044) 40191

Monaghan

St Davnet's Hospital Services Monaghan	(047) 81822

Roscommon

Addiction Counselling Service County Hospital	(0903) 26477

Sligo

Alcohol and Substance Counselling Sligo	(071) 43316

Tipperary

Aiseiri Cahir	(052) 41166
North Tipperary Community Services Nenagh	(067) 31800
South Tipperary Alcohol and Addiction Service Clonmel	(052) 26533
St Michael's Unit Clonmel	(052) 21900

Waterford

Accept: Addiction Treatment Service Cork Road, Waterford	(051) 54977
Waterford Drug Helpline Upper Yellow Road, Waterford	(051) 73333

Westmeath

Marist Rehabilitation Centre Athlone	(0902) 72035
Narcotics Anonymous Athlone	(0902) 74028

Wexford

Aiseiri Roxborough	(053) 41818
Counselling Service Enniscorthy	(054) 33110

How to get help in Britain

The best source of information in Britain for parents with concerns about drug use is from the National Drugs Helpline. This offers a twenty-four hour free service. It includes advice to families, to drug users, to friends or to anyone concerned. The helpline will give advice, information and counselling and even send you out brochures. It will also suggest referrals to appropriate agencies for you.

Tel No. (0800) 776600